T0387494

Earth Basics

Soil

by Rebecca Pettiford

Bullfrog Books

Ideas for Parents and Teachers

Bullfrog Books let children practice reading informational text at the earliest reading levels. Repetition, familiar words, and photo labels support early readers.

Before Reading

- Discuss the cover photo. What does it tell them?
- Look at the picture glossary together. Read and discuss the words.

Read the Book

- "Walk" through the book and look at the photos. Let the child ask questions. Point out the photo labels.
- Read the book to the child, or have him or her read independently.

After Reading

- Prompt the child to think more. Ask: Many plants need soil to grow. How does soil help plants grow?

Bullfrog Books are published by Jump!
5357 Penn Avenue South
Minneapolis, MN 55419
www.jumplibrary.com

Copyright © 2024 Jump! International copyright reserved in all countries. No part of this book may be reproduced in any form without written permission from the publisher.

Library of Congress Cataloging-in-Publication Data

Names: Pettiford, Rebecca, author.
Title: Soil / by Rebecca Pettiford.
Description: Minneapolis, MN: Jump!, Inc., [2024]
Series: Earth basics | Includes index.
Audience: Ages 5–8
Identifiers: LCCN 2022044306 (print)
LCCN 2022044307 (ebook)
ISBN 9798885244459 (hardcover)
ISBN 9798885244466 (paperback)
ISBN 9798885244473 (ebook)
Subjects: LCSH: Soils—Juvenile literature.
Classification: LCC S591.3 .P468 2024 (print)
LCC S591.3 (ebook)
DDC 631.4—dc23/eng/20221118
LC record available at https://lccn.loc.gov/2022044306
LC ebook record available at https://lccn.loc.gov/2022044307

Editor: Katie Chanez
Designer: Emma Almgren-Bersie

Photo Credits: ifong/Shutterstock, cover; Sofiia Tiuleneva/Shutterstock, 1; Serg64/Shutterstock, 3; VladGans/iStock, 4; Siam SK/Shutterstock, 5, 23br; Geri Lavrov/Getty, 6–7; stanley45/iStock, 8; greenaperture/Shutterstock, 9, 23tl; ThomasVogel/iStock, 10–11, 23bl, 23bm; laughingmango/iStock, 12–13; blickwinkel/Alamy, 14–15; Roman Pyshchyk/Shutterstock, 16; Drop of Light/Shutterstock, 17; caia image/Alamy, 18–19; delobol/Shutterstock, 20–21; Valentina Razumova/Shutterstock, 22tl; Alex Staroseltsev/Shutterstock, 22m; Kovaleva_Ka/Shutterstock, 22tr; Palo_ok/Shutterstock, 22bl; yevgeniy11/Shutterstock, 22bm; SeDmi/Shutterstock, 22br; J. Helgason/Shutterstock, 23tm; Sebastian Janicki/Shutterstock, 23tr; nito/Shutterstock, 24.

Printed in the United States of America at Corporate Graphics in North Mankato, Minnesota.

Table of Contents

Plant Time	4
Plants That Need Soil	22
Picture Glossary	23
Index	24
To Learn More	24

Plant Time

Ann digs a hole in the soil.

soil

Soil is the top layer of Earth.
It is made of rocks and minerals.

Plants need soil to grow.

Ann puts a plant in the soil.

Soil holds the water.

Roots absorb the water.

Water helps plants grow. Nutrients in soil do, too.

A mole digs.
This helps the soil.
How?
It puts holes in it.
Water can get to the roots.

Animals need plants to live. Rabbits eat them.

Deer do, too.

We eat plants, too!

Ann's plant grows berries.
Yum!
Let's plant more!

Plants That Need Soil

Almost all plants need soil to grow. What are some? Take a look!

Picture Glossary

absorb
To soak up liquid.

layer
A part of something that lies over or under another part.

minerals
Hard substances found on Earth that do not come from animals or plants.

nutrients
Substances that living things need to live and grow.

roots
Parts of plants that grow under the ground and collect water and nutrients.

soil
The top layer of Earth in which plants grow.

Index

animals 16
digs 4, 15
Earth 5
eat 16, 19
grow 6, 12, 20
minerals 5
nutrients 12
plants 6, 12, 16, 19, 20
rains 8
rocks 5
roots 11, 15
water 9, 11, 12, 15

To Learn More

Finding more information is as easy as 1, 2, 3.
① Go to www.factsurfer.com
② Enter "soil" into the search box.
③ Choose your book to see a list of websites.